HOLIDAY COUPETAILS

65 INSPIRED & FESTIVE RECIPES

BRIAN HART HOFFMAN
& BROOKE BELL

83 press

HOLIDAY
COUPETAILS

83 Press
2323 2nd Avenue North
Birmingham, AL 35203
83Press.com

ISBN 979-8-9874820-3-2
Printed in China

83
press

CONTENTS

INTRODUCTION

Our love for coupes began more than a decade ago when we began searching for antique glasses as we traveled, proudly displaying them on our home bars, and serving cocktails in them to family and friends. A cocktail in a coupe glass always feels more special!

The idea for this book was born on a cold and rainy day in London last December. We'd landed early in the morning and decided to fight jetlag by tucking into Dishoom's Kensington location. Dishoom is a fabulous Indian restaurant and just the comfort food we needed. It was packed with cheery holiday shoppers on a Sunday afternoon, so we waited at the bar for a table. Our blurry eyes glanced at the cocktail menu and quickly landed on their warm chai eggnog. One perfectly spiced sip, and we fell in love with the idea of eggnog being served warm.

Sometimes our brains work well through jetlag! Over our late afternoon Indian feast, we concepted the idea of a holiday cocktail book featuring our favorite coupe glass. And, we absolutely made a few more trips to Dishoom with friends, "for research." By the time we took a train to Paris a week later, we had an outline for this book and a lineup of recipes we couldn't wait to develop when we got home.

We hope this book will be your go-to guide for holiday entertaining and will spark your passion for starting a collection of coupe glasses or dusting off the set that might be packed up in your attic. There's no season better for cocktailing at home. Whether you like to host large gatherings or intimate dinner parties, these coupe cocktail recipes guarantee a joyous occasion.

It's not uncommon for Brian to say that "anything that holds liquid is a wine glass," and in the same spirit, any cocktail or beverage can be served in a coupe glass. It immediately makes it more festive and fun.

À la vôtre! (Cheers! To your health!)

—B+B

(Brian and Brooke)

THE
HOME
BAR

There's nothing more stylish than a home bar with a collected look that's full of personality. We love to display special bottles of wine and liquor, cut glass decanters, antique champagne buckets, bar tools, matches from favorite restaurants, and, of course, coupe glasses.

BRUNCH AND BE MERRY

Brunch is a low-stress way to entertain during the holidays, and a mimosa bar can take center stage. Pop the bubbly, juice some citrus, and throw in some fun options, such as pomegranate and cranberry. Everyone can serve themselves and enjoy the merriment of the season.

MAKE IT A JINGLE MINGLE

A good host always welcomes guests with a cocktail, and mixing a big batch of drinks gets one in their hands quickly. Use vintage pitchers and punch bowls for mixing and serving. We love picking up antique ladles at brocantes in France, keeping a few for ourselves and gifting others. Throughout the book, you'll see our Big Batch icon indicating recipes that are perfect for a crowd.

BIG BATCH

FIZZY & FESTIVE

'TIS THE SEASON TO
SPARKLE AND SHINE

Chapter

1

CAMPARI ROYALE

MAKES 1 SERVING

Aperol Spritz fans, don't come after me; I think they're too sweet.
I said what I said. While sitting for aperitivo in Roma (Rome), Italy,
and asking the bartender about making my spritz with
Campari to make it less sweet, he introduced me to the Campari Royale…
and my spritz life was born. —*Brian*

INGREDIENTS

1   ounce Campari
3 to 4 ounces cold Champagne
    or sparkling wine
3   dashes orange bitters*
Garnish: orange wedge

DIRECTIONS

1. Pour Campari into a coupe glass. Top with Champagne and orange bitters. Garnish with orange, if desired.

We used Angostura orange bitters.

KIR ROYALE WITH POMEGRANATE

MAKES 1 SERVING

This drink is associated with so many fun and festive memories, from sipping Kir Royale in the south of France with my Aunt Cheryl to Bastille Day lunches with Elizabeth Boldin Thomas. But the most special of them all is my wedding—Kir Royale was served to each guest as they arrived to set the tone for our celebration. Stephen and I opted for an "apéro hour" with our guests prior to the ceremony so the sunset could be enjoyed with one of our favorite bubbly drinks. —Brian

INGREDIENTS

1½ tablespoons
     pomegranate liqueur*
Fresh pomegranate seeds
4   ounces cold Champagne
     or sparkling wine

DIRECTIONS

1. In a coupe glass, add pomegranate liqueur and pomegranate seeds. Top with Champagne.

We used PAMA Pomegranate Liqueur.

FRENCH 75

MAKES 1 SERVING

Gin is not my thing. Being nervous isn't either. When Stephen and I went on our first date to Chez Fonfon in Birmingham, Alabama, the nerves caused me to order the first thing I saw on the drink menu—a French 75! I loved the drink and my date. I still don't love gin, but I will order one at Chez Fonfon to relive the memories of that very special day. —*Brian*

INGREDIENTS	DIRECTIONS
1 ounce gin ½ ounce freshly squeezed lemon juice ½ ounce Simple Syrup (recipe follows) 3 ounces cold Champagne or sparkling wine Garnish: lemon twist	1. In a cocktail shaker, add gin, lemon juice, and Simple Syrup. Add ice and shake until cold. Strain into a coupe glass. Top with Champagne. Garnish with lemon twist, if desired.

SIMPLE SYRUP

MAKES ABOUT 1 CUP

INGREDIENTS	DIRECTIONS
1 cup granulated sugar 1 cup water	1. In a small saucepan, bring sugar and 1 cup water to a boil until sugar dissolves. Let cool completely. Store, covered in an airtight jar, in refrigerator for up to 3 weeks.

WINTER SUNRISE

MAKES 1 SERVING

When I was a flight attendant, we made "sunrise" drinks with orange juice, cranberry juice, and club soda, so I decided this beverage needed an upgrade to first class with the addition of Champagne—and now my holidays are merry and bright! —Brian

INGREDIENTS

3 to 4 ounces cold Champagne or sparkling wine
1 ounce freshly squeezed mandarin juice
½ ounce 100% pure unsweetened cranberry juice
Garnish: mandarin orange slice

DIRECTIONS

1. In a coupe glass, add Champagne. Slowly add mandarin juice to the center of the glass. Slowly add cranberry juice to the center of the glass. Do not stir. Garnish with orange, if desired.

MISTLETOE MIMOSA

MAKES 1 SERVING

Mistletoe immediately calls a kiss to mind, and this mimosa will, too, when you pass over the Champagne with just a "kiss" of orange juice. —*Brian*

INGREDIENTS	DIRECTIONS
4 ounces cold Champagne or sparkling wine Squeeze of fresh orange juice, to taste	1. In a coupe glass, add Champagne. Top with squeeze of orange juice, to taste.

BUYING BUBBLES

When it comes to purchasing Champagne or sparkling wine for cocktail mixing, our advice is to always buy something that you would drink on its own. To us, quality does matter. We prefer Champagne, made from grapes grown in the Champagne region of France. If you're not able to find a reasonably priced Champagne, opt for a French Blanc de Blancs or Crémant. While Spanish Cava and Italian Prosecco are bubbly, we developed our cocktails with French Champagne and sparkling wines, which tend to be dry and less sweet.

POMEGRANATE MIMOSA

As you slide into the colder weather of winter, enjoy a sparkling drink that highlights the bright flavor of pomegranate. —B+B

SATSUMA MIMOSA

MAKES 1 SERVING

The holidays truly kick off when the first batch of Baldwin County, Alabama, satsumas are delivered to my house, sometimes in late October. For as long as the season runs, there will be satsumas in cocktails every night. I even freeze the juice in ice cube trays to get me through winter. —Brooke

INGREDIENTS	DIRECTIONS
½ ounce fresh satsuma or mandarin juice 4 ounces cold Champagne or sparkling wine	**1.** In a coupe glass, add satsuma juice. Top with Champagne.

INGREDIENTS

½   ounce pomegranate juice
4   ounces cold Champagne or
    sparkling wine
Garnish: fresh pomegranate seeds

DIRECTIONS

1. In a coupe glass, add pomegranate juice. Top with Champagne. Garnish with pomegranate seeds, if desired.

CRANBERRY MIMOSA

MAKES 1 SERVING

A quick splash of cranberry juice is all you need to liven up a mimosa and make it even more festive. —B+B

INGREDIENTS

½   ounce 100% pure
    unsweetened cranberry
    juice
4   ounces cold Champagne
    or sparkling wine
Garnish: frozen cranberries

DIRECTIONS

1. In a coupe glass, add cranberry juice. Top with Champagne. Garnish with frozen cranberries, if desired.

MERRY & BRIGHT

TOAST TO THE MOST
WONDERFUL TIME
OF THE YEAR

Chapter

2

CRANBERRY MANHATTAN

MAKES 1 SERVING

Manhattan's are "my drink"—especially when I am feeling fancy sitting at a restaurant or hotel bar. They're always served up, never on the rocks! For this festive take, I replaced the traditional Luxardo cherry garnish with a cranberry that's been sweetened in simple syrup. —Brian

INGREDIENTS

2   ounces bourbon
1   ounce sweet rouge vermouth*
2   teaspoons Cranberry Simple
     Syrup (recipe follows)
Garnish: cranberries (from
     Cranberry Simple Syrup)

DIRECTIONS

1. In a cocktail shaker, add bourbon, vermouth, and Cranberry Simple Syrup. Add ice and shake until cold. Strain into a coupe glass. Serve with cranberries, if desired.

*We used Dolin Rouge Vermouth de Chambéry Liqueur.

CRANBERRY SIMPLE SYRUP

MAKES ABOUT 3 CUPS

INGREDIENTS

2   cups frozen cranberries
1   cup granulated sugar
1   cup water

DIRECTIONS

1. In a medium saucepan over medium-high heat, bring cranberries, sugar, and 1 cup water to a boil. Reduce heat to low, and simmer for 10 minutes, stirring occasionally. If you cook longer, the cranberries will start to break down and lose their shape. Remove from heat; let cool completely. Transfer to a glass jar. Store, covered, in refrigerator for up to 2 weeks.

GIFT IT

Cocktail kits make great gifts for those hard-to-buy-for people on your list. Pair a jar of ruby-hued Cranberry Simple Syrup with a nice bottle of bourbon and vermouth, and the Manhattan lovers in your life will thank you every time cocktail hour rolls around.

STEPHEN'S MANHATTAN

MAKES 1 SERVING

While writing the recipes for this book, we asked my husband, Stephen, to share the recipe for his perfect Manhattan. Then we did "our thing" and created a cranberry version for a holiday twist. After thinking about how special his cocktail is to me, I decided to include it, too. It's the drink we serve the most at home—the one we greet guests with, the one we make for date night, and the one Stephen spent a lot of time perfecting. —Brian

INGREDIENTS	DIRECTIONS
2 ounces bourbon 1 ounce sweet rouge vermouth* Splash cherry liqueur* Garnish: maraschino cherries*	**1.** In a cocktail shaker, add bourbon, vermouth, and cherry liqueur. Add ice and shake until cold. Strain into a coupe glass. Serve with cherries, if desired. *We used Dolin Rouge Vermouth de Chambéry Liqueur and Luxardo Cherry Liqueur and Maraschino Cherries. NOTE: Be sure to store open vermouth in the refrigerator. It's also a good idea to write the date you opened it on the label.*

COSMOPOLITAN

MAKES 1 SERVING

*One sip, and you'll be transported back to a Sunday night in the '90s,
waiting for a new episode of* Sex in the City *to air on HBO. —B+B*

INGREDIENTS

1½ ounces vodka
1 ounce 100% pure unsweetened cranberry juice
1 ounce Grand Marnier
¼ ounce freshly squeezed lime juice
Garnish: lime zest curl and fresh cranberries

DIRECTIONS

1. In a cocktail shaker, add vodka, cranberry juice, Grand Marnier, and lime juice. Add ice and shake until cold. Strain into a coupe glass. Garnish with lime zest and fresh cranberries, if desired.

ELF ON THE TOP SHELF MARGARITA

MAKES 1 SERVING

Who says summer is margarita season? This refreshing holiday margarita is upvamped with Grand Marnier and a crave-worthy sweet-and-spicy rim. —*Brooke*

INGREDIENTS

1½ ounces tequila, plus more for rim
¼ cup superfine or granulated sugar
2 tablespoons kosher salt
2 teaspoons chili powder
1 ounce 100% pure unsweetened cranberry juice
1 ounce fresh lime juice
½ ounce Grand Marnier
½ ounce Simple Syrup (recipe on page 22)
Garnish: fresh lime

DIRECTIONS

1. On a small plate, place a small amount of tequila. On another small plate, combine sugar, salt, and chili powder. Dip rim of coupe glass in tequila and then in sugar mixture.

2. In a cocktail shaker, add tequila, cranberry juice, lime juice, Grand Marnier, and Simple Syrup. Add ice and shake until cold. Strain into prepared coupe glass. Garnish with lime, if desired.

GRINCH PUNCH

MAKES ABOUT 35 SERVINGS

One sip of this festive beverage will soften any grinch's heart, so queue up the original film from the 1960s and be ready for Whoville's happiness to spread into your home. I can't make this drink, watch the movie, or read the book without thinking of my good friend Jane Bertch. She is undoubtedly the biggest fan of the original film (no other versions exist in her mind—sorry, Jim Carrey!) and doesn't miss a chance to enjoy it each holiday season. Jane embodies the spirit of the Whos and sees the good in everyone and all situations, always reclaiming negative vibes and turning them into something to celebrate. Can't we all use more of that in the world? If you're feeling grinch-y, make this drink and find reasons to be festive, kind, and loving— in doing so, you might just soften another grinch's heart in the process! —Brian

BIG BATCH

INGREDIENTS

1 (½-gallon) container lime sherbet, melted
4 cups spicy ginger ale
4 cups pineapple juice
1½ cups vodka, plus more for rim
Garnish: red sprinkles*

DIRECTIONS

1. In a large serving bowl, add sherbet. Pour ginger ale, pineapple juice, and vodka on top, and stir to combine. Chill until ready to serve.

2. On a small plate, place a small amount of vodka. On another small plate, place sprinkles. Dip rim of coupe glass in vodka and then in sprinkles. Stir punch and ladle into prepared coupe glass.

We used Betty Crocker Red Sugar Sprinkles.

NOTE: Some brands of lime sherbet have a reaction with the acidity in the ginger ale and pineapple juice and may cause small blue particles to form. Don't freak out.

HOLIDAY SANGRIA

MAKES ABOUT 16 SERVINGS

Grandmillennials, your grandmother's punch bowl has never looked better!
Your holiday party needs this recipe. Since it only gets better with age,
mix up a batch the day before you plan to serve it so the flavors
have time to mix and mingle. —Brooke

INGREDIENTS

1   (750-mililiter) bottle dry
    red wine
½   cup Grand Marnier
½   cup brandy
2   cups fresh or frozen
    cranberries
1   orange, sliced
1   lemon, sliced
2   cinnamon sticks
4   star anise
4   springs fresh rosemary
½   liter sparkling water, chilled

DIRECTIONS

1. In a large container with a lid, add red wine, Grand Marnier, brandy, cranberries, orange slices, lemon slices, cinnamon sticks, star anise, and rosemary. Cover, and let chill overnight in the refrigerator. Before serving, remove cinnamon sticks and star anise, if desired. Stir in sparkling water. Ladle into coupe glasses.

NOTE: If you'd prefer to make this with white wine, choose one that is drier and more crisp, such as Sancerre or Sauvignon Blanc.

BAHAMIAN CHRISTMAS PUNCH

MAKES ABOUT 20 SERVINGS

Some of my favorite holidays have been spent in the Bahamas. One sip of this punch, and I am windblown on the pink sand beaches with turquoise water so bright it doesn't look real. This recipe is a rendition of the Goombay Smash you'll find throughout the islands. —*Brooke*

BIG BATCH

INGREDIENTS

2	cups coconut rum
2	cups dark rum
1	cup apricot brandy
3	cups pineapple juice
2	cups freshly squeezed
	orange juice

Garnish: fresh pineapple
    wedges and orange slices

DIRECTIONS

1. In a large pitcher, stir together coconut rum, dark rum, brandy, pineapple juice, and orange juice. Cover, and refrigerate until chilled. Pour into coupe glasses. Garnish with pineapple and orange, if desired.

BLOOD ORANGE NEGRONI

MAKES 1 SERVING

My forever favorite cocktail… The Negroni is one of those classics that you can order at any bar, anywhere. As long as the bartender knows the 1:1:1 ratio, it can't be messed up. But you can "plus it up" with fresh blood orange juice and good vermouth. —*Brooke*

INGREDIENTS

1   ounce gin
1   ounce Campari
1   ounce sweet rouge vermouth*
1   squeeze fresh blood
       orange juice
Garnish: dried blood orange slice

DIRECTIONS

1. In a cocktail shaker, add gin, Campari, vermouth, and blood orange juice. Add ice and shake until cold. Strain into a coupe glass. Garnish with dried blood orange, if desired.

*We used Dolin Rouge Vermouth de Chambéry Liqueur, which can be found in many grocery stores.

HOW TO MAKE DRIED CITRUS

To make dried citrus for cocktail garnishes, use a mandolin to carefully slice citrus ¼-inch thick. Place citrus slices on a parchment-lined baking pan. Bake at 175° until visibly dry and dehydrated, about 2 hours and 30 minutes. Be sure to check slices every 30 minutes.

Dried citrus can also give your holiday wreaths and garlands a festive touch and pop of color.

BOULEVARDIER

MAKES 1 SERVING

*Sometimes a drink tastes better when it's enjoyed in a specific place—and
Boulevardiers taste better when my friend Sam makes them. That's a fact,
but you can create your Boulevardier tradition with this recipe that's
perfectly adapted to drinking from a coupe once shaken until frosty
cold in lieu of the more traditional pour over ice.* —Brian

INGREDIENTS

1½   ounces rye whiskey*
1   ounce Campari
1   ounce sweet vermouth*
Garnish: orange twist

DIRECTIONS

1. In a cocktail shaker, add whiskey, Campari, and vermouth.
Add ice and shake until cold. Strain into a coupe glass. Garnish
with orange twist, if desired.

*We used Rittenhouse Rye Whiskey and Antica Formula
Carpano Vermouth.*

GARIBALDI

MAKES 1 SERVING

This classic cocktail is low-alcohol and perfect for day
drinking or when you're practicing moderation
in a season of indulgence. —B+B

INGREDIENTS	DIRECTIONS
2 ounces Campari 3 ounces freshly squeezed orange juice Garnish: orange wedge	**1.** In a cocktail shaker, add Campari and orange juice. Add ice and shake until cold. Strain into a coupe glass. Garnish with orange, if desired.

AULD LANG SYNE

MAKES 1 SERVING

Where do I begin with this cocktail? Let's start with my most favorite citrus, Alabama satsumas, or any satsumas for that matter. Small, thin-skinned, and sweet, they're amazing paired with vodka. Our local satsuma season ends close to the turn of the year, making this an ideal cocktail to sip for New Year's celebrations and reflections. I have a playlist that consists of nothing but Auld Lang Syne in as many versions as I can find, and it's on repeat for the last few days of each year as I take time to reflect on the previous year, seal memories in my mind, and look forward to the year ahead. From Mariah Carey's upbeat and humorous take to Kenny G's serenading saxophone, this cocktail pairs perfectly with any vibe you choose for your end-of-the-year celebration. —Brian

INGREDIENTS

2   ounces vodka
1   unpeeled satsuma or
    mandarin orange,
    quartered
Sparkling water

DIRECTIONS

1. In a cocktail shaker, muddle vodka and satsuma. Add ice and shake until cold. Strain into a coupe glass. Top with sparkling water.

SATSUMA CELEBRATION

We celebrate satsuma season from our first delivery in October until they go out of season after the holidays. They're plentiful along the Gulf Coast, and we ask anyone passing through the area to bring us a stash. Their thin skins are perfect for squeezing into cocktails, they rarely have seeds, and their juice is sweeter than oranges.

COMFORT & JOY

MAKE IT A DECEMBER
TO REMEMBER WITH
BOLD AND BOOZY
BEVERAGES

Chapter

3

SPICED & SPIKED APPLE CIDER

MAKES ABOUT 32 SERVINGS

Picture it: Homewood, Alabama, 2018. The weather turned cold with a brisk autumn wind the day of The Homewood Witches Ride, an annual Halloween fundraiser. I'd planned to sip on chilled wine. Instead, I made haste and quickly grabbed a bottle of spiced apple cider and heated it on the stovetop before adding a generous pour of bourbon to fill an insulated cup that would stay warm. One sip in as the witches took flight, and I knew it was an autumn warmer that would make a repeat appearance. Big batch and low stress, this seasonal delight wows the crowd. —Brian

BIG BATCH

INGREDIENTS

1 **gallon unfiltered spiced apple cider**
3 **cups bourbon**

DIRECTIONS

1. In a large saucepan or stockpot, add spiced apple cider and bourbon. Heat until mixture almost reaches a simmer. Do not boil. Serve warm.

NOTE: Be careful when adding hot liquids to very thin or antique coupe glasses.

VIN CHAUD

MAKES ABOUT 6 SERVINGS

If you ever get the chance to visit Strasbourg, France, and the famous holiday markets that transform the city into a holiday wonderland every December, you'll see large stockpots of vin chaud, *or hot mulled wine, everywhere you look. Steam billows into the cold air, and the smell of warm spices is intoxicating. When we visited to produce a holiday story for* Bake from Scratch *magazine, we warmed our hands between photos with cups of* vin chaud *served in the market's commemorative plastic cups. We think we nailed the recreation of our memory and can't wait to enjoy the elevated experience of sipping this drink in a beautiful coupe glass.* —B+B

BIG BATCH

INGREDIENTS

¼ cup mulling spice mix*
1 (750-mililiter) bottle dry red wine
¼ cup Grand Marnier
¼ cup granulated sugar
2 pieces orange peel
Garnish: dried orange slices (recipe on page 47)

DIRECTIONS

1. Cut a 9-inch square of cheesecloth. Add mulling spice mix to the center, and bring cheesecloth around spices to form a sachet. Tie with kitchen twine to secure, and trim excess cheesecloth.

2. In a large saucepan over low heat, add wine, Grand Marnier, sugar, orange peel, and spice mix. Heat until mixture almost reaches a simmer and sugar is dissolved. Do not boil. Let stand for 10 minutes. Remove spices before serving warm. Garnish with dried orange slices, if desired.

We used Penzy's Mulling Spices, which is a mix of whole cinnamon, cloves, allspice, cardamom, and mace.

Note: Be careful when adding hot liquids to very thin or antique coupe glasses.

HOT BUTTERED RUM

MAKES 1 SERVING

At the end of a long travel day, there's nothing better than dipping into a cozy hotel bar. You know the one… dark paneling with mood lighting set, cocktail shakers shaking, and the soothing hum of conversation amongst strangers. This cocktail helps us channel that hotel lounge vibe at home. And we finally have a reason to enjoy browned butter in liquid form. —B+B

INGREDIENTS	DIRECTIONS
4 ounces hot but not boiling water 2 tablespoons Browned Butter Sugar Mixture (recipe follows) 1½ ounces dark rum Garnish: cinnamon stick	1. In a heatproof mixing glass, add 4 ounces hot water, Browned Butter Sugar Mixture, and rum, stirring very well to combine. Pour into a coupe glass. Garnish with cinnamon stick, if desired. *NOTE: Be careful when adding hot liquids to very thin or antique coupe glasses.*

BROWNED BUTTER SUGAR MIXTURE

MAKES ENOUGH FOR ABOUT 4 COCKTAILS

INGREDIENTS	DIRECTIONS
½ cup unsalted butter ⅓ cup firmly packed light brown sugar 1 tablespoon pumpkin pie spice 1 teaspoon vanilla extract ¼ teaspoon kosher salt	1. In a medium saucepan, melt butter over medium heat. Cook, stirring frequently, until butter solids are golden and nutty in aroma, about 7 minutes. Strain through cheesecloth into a small bowl. Strain through cheesecloth again into another small bowl. (This will yield about ⅓ cup of browned butter.) 2. Refrigerate until firm, and then let stand at room temperature to soften for 30 minutes before using. Add sugar, pumpkin pie spice, vanilla, and salt to browned butter, stirring to combine. Store, covered, in refrigerator for up to 1 week.

RUM
OLD FASHIONED

MAKES 1 SERVING

Aged rum on the rocks, full of vanilla and caramel notes, is my ideal nightcap. And when it's turned into an old fashioned, you don't have to wait until the end of the evening to enjoy. Just stir and sip. —Brooke

INGREDIENTS	DIRECTIONS
1 ice sphere 3 ounces aged rum* ¼ ounce Simple Syrup (recipe on page 22) 2 dashes aromatic bitters 2 dashes orange bitters	**1.** In a coupe glass, add one ice sphere. In a mixing glass, add rum, Simple Syrup, aromatic bitters, and orange bitters. Stir to combine, and pour on top of ice. *Depending on the flavor of rum, you might need more or less Simple Syrup. Some aged rums are vanilla forward, so you won't need as much Simple Syrup.*

GINGER MEZCAL MULE

MAKES 1 SERVING

Mezcal is divisive. You either love it, or you hate it. I can't get enough of its smokiness, and when paired with spicy ginger beer, it gets even better. —Brooke

INGREDIENTS

4	ounces ginger beer
2	ounces mezcal
1	ounce fresh lime juice
Garnish: lime slice	

DIRECTIONS

1. In a mixing glass, add ginger beer, mezcal, and lime juice. Add ice and stir until cold. Strain into a coupe glass. Garnish with lime, if desired.

PECAN OLD FASHIONED

MAKES 1 SERVING

Or should it be called Pecan New Fashioned since we took this classic cocktail and served it up instead of on the rocks? Inspired by a Pecan Old Fashioned I enjoyed at Bottega in Birmingham, Alabama, the flavors of pecan and orange complement the bourbon to create a cozy cocktail that takes me back to mild autumn evenings on the patio at one of my favorite local restaurants. —Brian

INGREDIENTS

2   ounces bourbon
1   ounce pecan liqueur*
2   dashes aromatic bitters
Garnish: orange peel

DIRECTIONS

1. In a mixing glass, add bourbon, pecan liqueur, and bitters. Add ice and stir until cold. Strain into a coupe glass. Garnish with orange, if desired.

We used Rivulet Artisan Pecan Liqueur.

PEANUT BUTTER OLD FASHIONED

MAKES 1 SERVING

We'll never forget the unexpected pleasure of our first taste of peanut butter whiskey, otherwise known as Skrewball. After a long day on set producing videos for Bake from Scratch, our co-worker Jon Adamson pulled out a bottle of the peanut butter whiskey he'd been talking about for weeks. On the weekends, Jon and his wife, Michele, craft design Jello shots, so they're always experimenting with new flavor combinations. One sip of this velvet elixir, and we couldn't believe we were drinking boozy peanut butter. −B+B

INGREDIENTS

2	ounces bourbon
1	ounce peanut butter whiskey*
2	dashes aromatic bitters
2	dashes orange bitters

DIRECTIONS

1. In a mixing glass, add bourbon, peanut butter whiskey, aromatic bitters, and orange bitters. Add ice and stir until cold. Strain into coupe glass.

We used Skrewball.

GINGER GIN FIZZ

MAKES 1 SERVING

There are two secrets to this cocktail: the spicy Ginger Simple Syrup and the egg white. If you're wondering about the egg white, it's what gives a fizz cocktail its signature fizz. Splurge on good eggs and save your yolks for eggnog. —*Brooke*

INGREDIENTS	DIRECTIONS
3 ounces gin*	**1.** In a cocktail shaker, add gin, Ginger Simple Syrup, egg white, and lime juice. Add ice and shake until cold. Strain into a coupe glass. Top with club soda.
1 ounce Ginger Simple Syrup (recipe follows)	
1 large egg white	*We used Hendrick's Gin.*
½ teaspoon fresh lime juice	
1 ounce club soda	

GINGER SIMPLE SYRUP

MAKES ABOUT ¾ CUP

INGREDIENTS	DIRECTIONS
1 cup granulated sugar	**1.** In a small saucepan, whisk sugar, 1 cup water, and ginger until combined. Bring to boil over medium heat, reduce heat to a simmer, and let mixture cook for 15 minutes. Let cool completely. Strain, and discard ginger. Store, covered in an airtight container, in refrigerator for up to 3 weeks.
1 cup water	
1 cup fresh ginger, peeled and chopped	

SNOWY & WHITE

POUR A COZY DRINK
AND HAVE YOURSELF
A MERRY LITTLE
CHRISTMAS

Chapter

4

BRIAN'S CLASSIC EGGNOG COUPETAIL

MAKES 1 SERVING

I owe my love for eggnog to my late grandmother, Mimi. Each year, as soon as the Barber's eggnog hit the grocery store shelves, she'd have it on hand throughout the festive season. She didn't add anything to it, as her love for something sweet was as permanent as her smile. My love for eggnog took me on the path to creating my own recipe. When I shared mine with Mimi and she loved it, I knew it would be a hit. For more than a decade, I've been making big batches of eggnog and gifting it to family and friends in a French milk bottle. Each year, I collect the empty bottles and refill them. Now, you can use this recipe for gifting, entertaining, or, like my Mimi would, for her own enjoyment. —Brian

INGREDIENTS

4 ounces Brian's Eggnog (recipe follows)
1 ounce bourbon
½ ounce brandy
Garnish: freshly grated nutmeg

DIRECTIONS

1. In a cocktail shaker, add Brian's Eggnog, bourbon, and brandy. Add ice and shake until cold. Strain into a coupe glass. Garnish with nutmeg, if desired.

BRIAN'S EGGNOG

MAKES ABOUT 4 CUPS

INGREDIENTS

1½ cups heavy whipping cream
⅔ cup granulated sugar
4 large eggs
2 large egg yolks
1½ cups cold whole milk
½ teaspoon freshly grated nutmeg

DIRECTIONS

1. In a large saucepan, bring cream to a simmer over medium heat.

2. Meanwhile, in a medium bowl, whisk together the sugar, eggs, and egg yolks until light and pale. Gradually whisk the hot cream into the egg mixture. Add mixture back to saucepan, and cook over medium-low heat, whisking constantly, until the mixture is thick enough to coat the back of a spoon and registers 140°F on an instant-read thermometer. Remove from heat, and immediately strain into a bowl. Stir in milk and nutmeg. Refrigerate to chill. Store, covered, in refrigerator, for up to 4 days.

FROZEN BOURBON MILK PUNCH

MAKES ABOUT 20 SERVINGS

*My first sip of this cold and delicious beverage was also during my first visit to
St. Francisville, Louisiana, for a pre-wedding celebration for my twin brother,
Eric, and his then fiancé, Katie—and it was immediate love… not just for
the drink, but for my "SIL" (sister-in-law), too. Since then, it's a holiday
beverage that Katie makes for friends and neighbors as bottled gifts!
As they say in Louisiana, "laissez les bon temps rouler!"* —Brian

BIG BATCH

INGREDIENTS

8   cups vanilla bean ice
    cream, melted
2   cups bourbon
3   tablespoons vanilla extract
Garnish: freshly grated nutmeg

DIRECTIONS

1. In a large container with a lid, add ice cream, bourbon, and
vanilla. Stir until combined. Store, covered, in freezer until ready
to serve. Scoop into a chilled coupe glass. Garnish with nutmeg,
if desired.

IRISH CREAM

MAKES 5½ CUPS

My mom makes and gifts Irish Cream every Christmas, and this recipe is very close to hers. I love when her bottles, tied with fresh greenery and kumquats, make their way to my house. Stashing it in the freezer to get slushy is highly recommended. —*Brooke*

BIG
BATCH

INGREDIENTS

2   cups heavy whipping
     cream
2   cups Irish whiskey
1   (14-ounce) can sweetened
     condensed milk
2   tablespoons instant
     espresso powder
2   teaspoons vanilla extract

DIRECTIONS

1. In a large bowl, whisk together cream, whiskey, condensed milk, espresso powder, and vanilla. Chill completely. To serve, pour into a coupe glass. Store, in an airtight container, in refrigerator for up to 1 week.

You can place in the freezer for about 4 hours for a slushy consistency.

SNOWSTORM WHITE RUSSIAN

MAKES 1 SERVING

I remember my parents making White Russians when I was a child. It was a magical, ethereal elixir I couldn't wait to enjoy as an adult. They still seem special to me, and I always smile when I see one being served. —*Brooke*

INGREDIENTS

3 ounces vodka, plus more for rim
¼ cup granulated sugar
¼ teaspoon espresso powder
2 ounces heavy whipping cream
1½ ounces coffee liqueur*

DIRECTIONS

1. On a small plate, add a small amount of vodka. On a another small plate, combine sugar and espresso powder. Dip rim of coupe glass in vodka and then sugar mixture.

2. In a cocktail shaker, add vodka and cream. Add ice and shake until cold. Strain into prepared coupe glass. Slowly add coffee liqueur to the center of the glass to create a stunning color gradient. Stir before serving.

We used Kahlúa.

NOTE: For an even more festive take on this classic, substitute eggnog for the heavy whipping cream.

RUMCHATA

MAKES 1 SERVING

*We can't mix this cocktail without singing, "In December drinking horchata,"
the first line of Vampire Weekend's song "Horchata." This is quite
possibly one of our favorite drinks included in this book. The Horchata
is indulgent on its own, but even better with rum. —B+B*

INGREDIENTS	DIRECTIONS
1½ ounces aged rum 3 ounces Horchata (recipe follows) Garnish: ground cinnamon	1. In a cocktail shaker, add rum and Horchata. Add ice and shake until cold. Strain into a coupe glass. Garnish with ground cinnamon, if desired.

HORCHATA

MAKES ABOUT 4½ CUPS

INGREDIENTS	DIRECTIONS
1 cup long-grain white rice, rinsed 2 cinnamon sticks, broken into pieces 4 cups hot water 1 (14-ounce) can sweetened condensed milk 1 cup unsweetened almond milk 1 tablespoon vanilla extract	1. In a large bowl, place uncooked rice, cinnamon sticks, and 4 cups hot water. Cover, and let stand in refrigerator overnight. 2. In a blender, add rice mixture (including the pieces of cinnamon stick). Process until smooth. Strain mixture through a fine-mesh sieve into a medium bowl, using a spatula to press out all liquid. Add condensed milk, almond milk, and vanilla, whisking until combined. Cover, and let mixture chill completely in refrigerator. Use within 3 or 4 days, and whisk well before using.

WARM CHAI EGGNOG

MAKES 1 SERVING

The idea of this book was born after we enjoyed a warm chai eggnog at Dishoom in London last December. We loved how it was lightly spiced and served warm. Each sip takes us back to a table full of best baking friends and lots of laughs. —Brian

INGREDIENTS

4   ounces warm Chai Eggnog
     (recipe follows)
1   ounce dark rum*
Garnish: ground cardamom

DIRECTIONS

1. In a mixing glass, add Chai Eggnog and rum. Pour into a coupe glass, and serve warm. Garnish with cardamom, if desired.

We used Gosling Black Seal Rum.

Note: Be careful when adding hot liquids to very thin or antique coupe glasses.

CHAI EGGNOG

MAKES ABOUT 4 CUPS

INGREDIENTS

1½   cups whole milk
4   vanilla-chai black
     tea bags*
1½   cups heavy
     whipping cream
⅔   cup granulated
     sugar
4   large eggs
2   large egg yolks

DIRECTIONS

1. In a large saucepan, bring milk to a simmer over medium heat. Pour into a heat-proof measuring cup. Add tea bags, and let steep.

2. In the same saucepan, bring cream to a simmer over medium heat. Meanwhile, in a medium bowl, whisk together the sugar, eggs, and egg yolks until light and pale. Gradually whisk the hot cream into the egg mixture. Add mixture back to saucepan, and cook over low heat, whisking constantly, until the mixture is thick enough to coat the back of a spoon and registers 140°F on an instant-read thermometer. Remove from heat, and immediately strain into a bowl. Stir in chai-infused milk, gently pressing tea bags with a spatula to remove milk and flavor. Store, covered, in refrigerator, for up to 3 days. Warm before using.

We used Bigelow Vanilla Chai Black Tea.

WHITE CHRISTMAS BRANDY ALEXANDER

MAKES 1 SERVING

One mention of a Brandy Alexander when my twin brother, Eric, and I were with our mom, and the giggles begin all over again. You see, this giggle fest began on the high seas during a family trip to Bermuda when mom enjoyed a Brandy Alexander before dinner. When asked if she would like another, Eric and I answered on her behalf with a resounding yes! Rare was it that she would sip two cocktails in a row, so you can only imagine how we all laughed as she sipped on her second—and I can still hear that giggly laugh from that evening. It was so fun. My mom absolutely loved watching White Christmas *every year, so in her memory, I will do the same. I will sip on one (maybe two!) of these Brandy Alexanders from the coupe glasses you see in the photograph. They were her glasses, and I have cherished them from the day she passed them on to me. —Brian*

INGREDIENTS	DIRECTIONS
1½ ounces brandy 1 ounce crème de cacao liqueur 1 ounce heavy whipping cream Garnish: freshly ground nutmeg	1. In a cocktail shaker, add brandy, crème de cacao liqueur, and cream. Add ice and shake until cold. Strain into a coupe glass. Garnish with nutmeg, if desired.

PEPPERMINT BARK COCKTAIL

MAKES 1 SERVING

When Williams Sonoma introduced Peppermint Bark, a confection created using layers of milk or dark chocolate, white chocolate, and crushed peppermint candy, the craze began. December 1st is National Peppermint Bark Day and a great day to enjoy this cocktail with a tin of the beloved bark. —Brian

INGREDIENTS

1 ounce vanilla-flavored vodka, plus more for rim
Crushed hard peppermint candies
1 ounce white chocolate liqueur*
1 ounce heavy whipping cream
½ ounce peppermint schnapps
1 ounce milk chocolate liqueur*

DIRECTIONS

1. On a small plate, place a small amount of vodka. On another small plate, place crushed peppermint. Dip rim of coupe glass in vodka and then in peppermint.

2. In a cocktail shaker, add vodka, white chocolate liqueur, cream, and schnapps. Add ice and shake until cold. Strain into prepared coupe glass. Slowly pour milk chocolate liqueur into center of glass to create a layered cocktail. Stir before serving, if desired.

We used Mozart White and Milk Chocolate Liqueur.

NUTTY IRISHMAN

MAKES 1 SERVING

Part nutty, part Irish, this boozy after-dinner drink is all good.
We love Five Farms Irish Cream, which is made in County Cork,
Ireland, where the cows are happy, grazing verdant hills,
and the cream is sourced from family-owned farms. —B+B

INGREDIENTS	DIRECTIONS
2 ounces hazelnut liqueur* 2 ounces Irish cream*	1. In a mixing glass, add hazelnut liqueur and Irish Cream. Add ice and stir until cold. Strain into a coupe glass. *We used Frangelico Hazelnut Liqueur and Five Farms Irish Cream. Be sure to store the Irish cream in the refrigerator after opening.

SUGAR COOKIE FOR "SANTA"

MAKES 1 SERVING

Santa will appreciate this cocktail being left with his plate of cookies. It's just the fuel he needs to blitz around the world in one night delivering presents. —B+B

INGREDIENTS

1½ ounces vanilla-flavored vodka, plus more for rim

Red and green sanding sugars

1 ounce Irish cream

1 ounce heavy whipping cream

¼ ounce almond-flavored liqueur*

DIRECTIONS

1. On a small plate, add a small amount of vanilla-flavored vodka. On another small plate, add sugars in quadrants to create a checkerboard. Dip rim of coupe glass in vodka and then sugars.

2. In a cocktail shaker, add vodka, Irish cream, cream, and almond-flavored liquer. Add ice and shake until cold. Strain into a coupe glass.

We used Disaronno.

NAUGHTY
& NICE

BRING A LITTLE JOY TO
YOUR WORLD WITH
THESE COMFORTING
COCKTAILS

Chapter

5

HOT CHOCOLATE COUPETAIL

MAKES 1 SERVING

If you hang out at the bar at Gramercy Tavern in New York City enough and ask enough questions about their amazing Hot Chocolate Martini, you might just glean enough information to recreate it. Or just make this recipe… because I did all of the nosey work for you! There's something so chic and unique about a warm beverage served in a coupe on a cold winter night. Enjoy it for dessert or a nightcap! —Brian

INGREDIENTS	DIRECTIONS
3 ounces warm Hot Chocolate (recipe follows) 1 ounce vanilla-flavored vodka 1 ounce amaro*	**1.** In a mixing glass, add Hot Chocolate, vodka, and amaro. Stir until combined. Pour into a coupe glass. *We used Amaro Montenegro.* Note: Be careful when adding hot liquids to very thin or antique coupe glasses.

HOT CHOCOLATE

MAKES ABOUT 3½ CUPS

INGREDIENTS	DIRECTIONS
3 ounces 64% cocoa chocolate, chopped* 4 ounces 46% cocoa chocolate, chopped* 1 cup whole milk 1 cup heavy whipping cream ⅓ cup Dutch process cocoa powder* 1 teaspoon cornstarch ½ teaspoon ground cinnamon ¼ teaspoon kosher salt 2 teaspoons granulated sugar 1 tablespoon vanilla extract	**1.** In a medium bowl, place chopped chocolate. **2.** In a medium saucepan, whisk milk, cream, cocoa powder, cornstarch, cinnamon, salt, and sugar to combine. Cook over medium heat, stirring constantly, until mixture comes to a boil. Reduce heat, and let simmer for 2 to 3 minutes, stirring constantly. Remove from heat, and pour over chopped chocolate. Let stand for 2 minutes, and whisk mixture until smooth and combined. Add vanilla, whisking to combine. Unused hot chocolate can be stored in the refrigerator. Place plastic wrap directly on surface to prevent a skin from forming. *We used Guittard Chocolate and Cocoa Rouge Cocoa Powder.*

PEANUT BUTTER HOT CHOCOLATE

MAKES 1 SERVING

Is there anything more to say about this drink that the title doesn't explain? And cheers to the genius that created peanut butter whiskey… our hot chocolate thanks you. —Brian

INGREDIENTS

3   ounces warm Hot Chocolate (recipe on page 96)
2   ounces peanut butter whiskey*
Chocolate Peanut Butter Fudge, to serve (recipe on page 122)

DIRECTIONS

1. In a mixing glass, add Hot Chocolate and peanut butter whiskey. Stir until combined. Pour into a coupe glass. Serve with Chocolate Peanut Butter Fudge, if desired.

*We used Skrewball.

NOTE: Be careful when adding hot liquids to very thin or antique coupe glasses.

POLAR ESPRESSOTINI

MAKES 1 SERVING

The Espresso Martini is the cocktail world's current comeback kid and having quite the moment. Since this cocktail has some "pickup," we have rules. We don't drink one after 4:00 p.m. because sleep is too precious. And always add Irish cream. Thank you for coming to our Ted Talk. —B+B

INGREDIENTS

2   ounces vodka, plus more for rim
¼   cup granulated sugar
1   teaspoon espresso powder
1   ounce freshly brewed espresso, cooled
½   ounce coffee liqueur
½   ounce Irish cream
½   ounce Simple Syrup (recipe on page 22)

DIRECTIONS

1. On a small plate, add a small amount of vodka. On another small plate, combine sugar and espresso powder. Dip rim of coupe glass in vodka and then sugar mixture.

2. In a cocktail shaker, add vodka, cooled espresso, coffee liqueur, Irish cream, and Simple Syrup. Add ice and shake until cold. Strain into prepared coupe glass.

GRASSHOPPER

MAKES 1 SERVING

I don't know that I've actually ever seen my mother drink a Grasshopper, but she loves to talk about this after-dinner drink and how good they used to be. I hope this iteration will win her approval and bring back minty memories. —*Brooke*

INGREDIENTS

2   ounces vodka
1   ounce white chocolate
    liqueur*
1   ounce heavy whipping
    cream
½   ounce green crème de
    menthe
Garnish: whipped cream
    and fresh mint

DIRECTIONS

1. In a cocktail shaker, add vodka, white chocolate liqueur, cream, and crème de menthe. Add ice and shake until cold. Strain into a coupe glass. Garnish with whipped cream and mint, if desired.

We used White Chocolate Liqueur.

GINGERBREAD EGGNOG

MAKES 1 SERVING

If you're looking for a taste of the season, this is it! Seriously. This cocktail combines eggnog with a simple syrup that tastes just like a gingerbread cookie and will make your kitchen smell amazing. And for good measure, we decided to serve it with an actual gingerbread cookie. Merry cocktailing! —B+B

INGREDIENTS

1½ ounces aged rum, plus more for rim
Turbinado sugar
3 ounces Brian's Eggnog (recipe on page 74)
1 ounce Gingerbread Simple Syrup (recipe follows)
Garnish: Iced Gingerbread Cookie (recipe on page 126)

DIRECTIONS

1. On a small plate, add a small amount of rum. On another small plate, add turbinado sugar. Dip rim of coupe glass in rum and then sugar.

2. In a cocktail shaker, add rum, Brian's Eggnog, and Gingerbread Simple Syrup. Add ice and shake until cold. Strain into a coupe glass. Garnish with Iced Gingerbread Cookie, if desired.

GINGERBREAD SIMPLE SYRUP

MAKES ABOUT 1 CUP

INGREDIENTS

¾ cup water
½ cup firmly packed dark brown sugar
¼ cup unsulphured molasses
1 teaspoon ground ginger
1 teaspoon ground cinnamon
¼ teaspoon ground cardamom
⅛ teaspoon ground nutmeg
1 teaspoon vanilla extract

DIRECTIONS

1. In a medium saucepan over medium-high heat, add ¾ cup water, sugar, molasses, ginger, cinnamon, cardamom, and nutmeg and bring to a boil, whisking occasionally. Reduce heat to low, and simmer until sugar is dissolved.

2. Remove from heat, and add vanilla extract, whisking to combine. Let cool completely. Transfer to a glass jar. Store, covered, in refrigerator for up to 2 weeks.

BOOZY SIPPING CHOCOLATE

MAKES 1 SERVING

The only way we know of to make the lusciously thick hot chocolate found in Paris better is to spike it. You can make it boozy and better with the addition of Grand Marnier. Et violà! —B+B

INGREDIENTS	DIRECTIONS
3 ounces hot Sipping Chocolate (recipe follows) 1 ounce Grand Marnier Garnish: orange peel	**1.** In a mixing glass, combine Sipping Chocolate and Grand Marnier. Pour into coupe glass. Garnish with orange peel, if desired. *NOTE: We also tested this recipe with 1 ounce of Luxardo Cherry Liqueur and Maraschino Cherries in place of the Grand Marnier and orange peel, and it's equally fabulous.* *NOTE: Be careful when adding hot liquids to very thin or antique coupe glasses.*

SIPPING CHOCOLATE

MAKES ENOUGH FOR ABOUT 5 SERVINGS

INGREDIENTS	DIRECTIONS
1 cup whole milk ½ cup heavy whipping cream 8 ounces 60%-70% chocolate, chopped ½ teaspoon vanilla extract	**1.** In a small saucepan, add milk and cream. Heat over low heat just until it's about to come to a simmer. Do not boil. Add chocolate and vanilla, and whisk until melted and combined (mixture will be thick). Keep hot for serving.

SIP & SAVOR

FESTIVE BITES TO SERVE ALONGSIDE YOUR COUPETAIL

Chapter

6

PARMESAN AND CHIVE GOUGÈRES

MAKES ABOUT 38

One bite of gougère, and we have instant comfort and lots of memories. We learned to make them by hand at The Cook's Atelier in Beaune, France. And we'll never forget arriving at Dorie Greenspan's Paris apartment for a dinner party and being welcomed by gougère, hot from the oven. Whenever we serve them to friends and family for apéro, the cloud-like puffs disappear in no time. —B+B

INGREDIENTS

- ½ cup (113 grams) unsalted butter, cubed
- ½ cup (120 grams) water
- ½ cup (120 grams) whole milk
- 2 teaspoons (8 grams) granulated sugar
- 1 teaspoon (3 grams) kosher salt
- 1 cup (125 grams) all-purpose flour
- 5 large eggs (250 grams), room temperature
- 1⅓ cups (114 grams) finely grated Parmesan cheese, divided
- ¼ cup plus 2 tablespoons (18 grams) finely chopped fresh chives, divided

DIRECTIONS

1. Preheat oven to 375°F (190°C). Line 2 to 3 baking sheets with parchment paper.

2. Using a permanent marker and a 2-inch round cutter as a guide, draw circles at least 1½ inches apart on another sheet of parchment paper; slide template under parchment on a prepared pan.

3. In a medium saucepan, bring butter, ½ cup (120 grams) water, milk, sugar, and salt to a rolling boil over medium-high heat. Using a wooden spoon, stir in flour. Cook, stirring constantly, until a skin forms on the bottom of pan and mixture pulls away from the sides, forming a ball, 1 to 2 minutes.

4. Transfer mixture to the bowl of a stand mixer fitted with the paddle attachment; beat at low speed until dough cools slightly, 30 seconds to 1 minute. Add eggs, one at a time, beating until combined after each addition. (Batter will be shiny and will slowly move back together when a spatula is dragged through it.) Add ⅔ cup (57 grams) cheese and ¼ cup (12 grams) chives, and beat at low speed until combined.

5. Transfer batter to a large pastry bag fitted with a ½-inch round piping tip (Wilton #1A). Place piping tip in center of a drawn circle. Hold tip perpendicular ½ inch above parchment paper. Holding tip stationary the entire time, apply even pressure until batter reaches edges of drawn circle. Stop applying pressure and move tip in a quick circular motion as you lift away to help prevent a point from forming on top. Repeat with remaining batter until pan is full. Wet your finger with water, and press down any points to create a smooth top, if necessary. Slide template out from under piped batter, and place under parchment on other prepared pans; pipe remaining batter.

6. Bake, in batches, for 10 minutes. Rotate pans, and bake until fully puffed and deep golden brown, 10 to 15 minutes more. Garnish with remaining ⅔ cup (57 grams) cheese and remaining 2 tablespoons (6 grams) chives. Serve warm or at room temperature. Best served same day.

SAVORY SHORTBREAD COINS

MAKES 24

Sweet and nutty Asiago pairs perfectly with pecans and earthy sage. Be sure to make extra because you'll want these to stick around —B+B

INGREDIENTS

- ½ cup (113 grams) unsalted butter, softened
- 1 cup (99 grams) packed finely shredded Asiago cheese
- 2 tablespoons (14 grams) finely chopped pecans*
- 1 teaspoon minced fresh sage
- ½ teaspoon (1.5 grams) kosher salt
- ½ teaspoon (1 gram) ground black pepper
- 1¼ cups (156 grams) all-purpose flour
- 1 large egg white (30 grams), whisked

Garnish: fresh sage leaves

DIRECTIONS

1. In the bowl of a stand mixer fitted with the paddle attachment, beat butter at medium speed until creamy, about 1 minute. Add Asiago, pecans, sage, salt, and pepper, beating until combined. With mixer on low speed, gradually add flour, beating until large clumps form, 2 to 3 minutes. Turn out dough, and gently knead until no longer crumbly. Shape into a 9½-inch-long log. Wrap in plastic wrap, and freeze for 1 hour.

2. Preheat oven to 350°F (180°C). Line a baking sheet with parchment paper.

3. Trim ¼ inch from each end; discard. Cut log into 24 (⅜-inch-thick) slices. Place about 1 inch apart on prepared pan. Brush with egg white. Top with sage, if desired.

4. Bake until very lightly browned on bottom, 18 to 20 minutes. Let cool completely on pan. Store in an airtight container for up to 2 weeks.

We love using Georgia-grown Schermer Pecans.

MINI ECCLES CAKES WITH ENGLISH CHEDDAR

MAKES 14

Recipe adapted from Leiths Cookery Bible *by Prue Leith and Caroline Waldegrave*

To know Eccles cakes is to love Eccles cakes. We first tasted them at Pump Street Bakery in the seaside village of Orford, England, when we were producing a British issue of Bake from Scratch *magazine. We continued our love affair with them at Leiths Cookery School in London, where we learned to bake these beautiful bites that are best served with a knob of Lancashire cheese from Neal's Yard Dairy.* —B+B

INGREDIENTS

¼ cup (55 grams) firmly packed light brown sugar

2 tablespoons (28 grams) unsalted butter, cubed

1 teaspoon (1 gram) lemon zest

1 tablespoon (15 grams) fresh lemon juice

¼ teaspoon ground cinnamon

¼ teaspoon ground ginger

⅛ teaspoon ground nutmeg

⅛ teaspoon kosher salt

¾ cup (100 grams) sweetened dried currents or raisins, coarsely chopped

¼ cup (41 grams) candied orange peel or mixed peel, finely chopped

1 large egg yolk (20 grams), room temperature

1 teaspoon (15 grams) water

Rough Puff Pastry Dough (recipe on page 131)

2 tablespoons (24 grams) caster or superfine sugar

Sliced English Cheddar, to serve

DIRECTIONS

1. Preheat oven to 400°F (200°C). Line a baking sheet with parchment paper.

2. In a small saucepan, melt sugar, butter, lemon zest, lemon juice, cinnamon, ginger, nutmeg, and salt over medium heat until sugar is dissolved. Remove from heat.

3. In a medium bowl, combine currants and orange peel. Pour in butter mixture; toss to combine.

4. In a small bowl, whisk together egg yolk and 1 teaspoon (15 grams) water.

5. On a lightly floured surface, roll Rough Puff Pastry Dough to a ¼-inch thick rectangle (16x12-inches). Using a 3-inch round cutter dipped in flour, cut out 14 circles (discard scraps). Place 1 tablespoon (14 grams) filling into the center of each circle. Brush egg wash along the edges of each circle. Gather and pinch edges up and around filling until well-sealed (it will now be a round dough ball). Place seam side down, and using a rolling pin or hands, gently flatten pastries into even disks. Place about 1½ inches apart on prepared pan. Refrigerate until firm, 10 to 15 minutes. Using a small, sharp knife, make three cuts on top of the pastries. Brush with egg wash and sprinkle with caster sugar.

6. Bake until edges are golden brown, 10 to 13 minutes. Transfer to wire rack to cool. Enjoy warm or room temperature. Serve with English Cheddar, if desired. Best served same day.

CITRUS OLIVES

MAKES 4 CUPS

My husband Andy and I have always enjoyed picnics, but go ahead and erase the vision of red-checked tablecloths. On our first wedding anniversary trip to Napa Valley more than 15 years ago, one of our favorite nights was a "picnic night" at the cottage where we were staying. Sure, we loved eating at the area's fabulous restaurants, but the night we lit a fire in the fireplace, steamed artichokes, and spread out local cheeses, charcuterie, and marinated olives on the coffee table stands out most in my mind. Fast forward to a few years ago when we were in Burgundy, France. We spent days driving the countryside as Andy checked off seeing every Grand Cru vineyard in the Côtes-de-Nuits. I was along for the ride, and the picnics. I love that it's completely normal in France to pull off on the side of the road, find a nice shade tree, open a bottle of wine, and set out a picnic. Citrus Olives have always been part of our vineyard picnics. —Brooke

INGREDIENTS

2   tablespoons (30 grams) olive oil
3   garlic cloves (10 grams), thinly sliced
½   teaspoon fennel seeds
2   bay leaves
10   (½-inch wide) strips lemon zest (8 grams)
10   (1-inch wide) strips orange zest (18 grams)
¼   teaspoon crushed red pepper
3   springs fresh thyme
2   (8-ounce) jars (452 grams) Castelvetrano olives, drained
1   (9.5-ounce) jar (269 grams) kalamata olives, drained
⅓   cup (86 grams) drained sweet drop peppers
1   tablespoon (15 grams) fresh lemon juice

DIRECTIONS

1. In a large sauté pan, heat olive oil over medium heat. Add garlic, fennel seeds, and bay leaves. Cook, stirring occasionally, until aromatic and lightly golden, about 5 minutes.

2. Remove pan from heat and stir in zests, crushed red pepper, and thyme. Add drained olives, peppers, and lemon juice; stir to combine. Serve warm or at room temperature. Store in airtight container in refrigerator for up to two weeks.

CHINESE FIVE SPICE HAYSTACKS

MAKES 24

I loved when my mom made haystacks when I was a kid. To this day, the crunchy meets sweet treats are special. I decided to put my twist on the classic by adding Chinese five spice and flaked sea salt. Now they're next-level good. —*Brian*

INGREDIENTS

- 1   cup (150 grams) chopped white chocolate
- ⅔   cup (120 grams) butterscotch chips
- ¼   cup (66 grams) unsweetened creamy peanut butter
- 3   cups (168 grams) chow mein noodles
- ½   cup (76 grams) roasted and salted peanuts
- 1   teaspoon (2 grams) Chinese five spice

Garnish: flaked sea salt

DIRECTIONS

1. In the top of a double boiler, add white chocolate, butterscotch chips, and peanut butter. Heat, stirring occasionally, until melted and smooth, 2 to 3 minutes.

2. Remove from heat and stir in chow mein noodles, peanuts, and Chinese five spice.

3. Line a rimmed baking sheet with parchment paper. Drop 1½ tablespoon-sized (about 27 grams) mounds of mixture onto prepared tray (mixing, as needed, if chocolate starts to settle in bottom of bowl). Garnish with flaked sea salt, if desired. Refrigerate until coating is set, about 15 minutes. Store in an airtight container at room temperature for up to 1 week.

MULLED WINE BROWNIE BITES

MAKES 24

Sometimes we drink wine and eat chocolate. Sometimes we bake and drink wine. And sometimes we need wine and chocolate in our baking. —*B+B*

INGREDIENTS

- ⅓ cup (42 grams) all-purpose flour
- ⅓ cup (26 grams) unsweetened cocoa powder
- ½ teaspoon (1.5 grams) kosher salt
- ½ teaspoon (1 grams) ground cinnamon
- ¼ teaspoon ground ginger
- ⅛ teaspoon ground nutmeg
- ⅛ teaspoon ground cloves
- ⅛ teaspoon ground allspice
- ⅛ teaspoon ground black pepper
- 1 cup (220 grams) firmly packed light brown sugar
- 1 large egg (50 grams), room temperature
- 1 large egg yolk (19 grams), room temperature
- 5 ounces (142 grams) bittersweet 60% cocoa chocolate, chopped and divided
- ⅓ cup (76 grams) unsalted butter, cubed
- 3 tablespoons (60 grams) Vin Chaud (recipe on page 59)
- 1 teaspoon (4 grams) vanilla extract
- ½ teaspoon orange zest
- ¼ cup (60 grams) heavy whipping cream

Garnish: confectioners' sugar

DIRECTIONS

1. Preheat oven to 350°F (180°C). Lightly spray a 24-cup mini muffin pan with baking spray with flour.

2. In a medium bowl, whisk together flour, cocoa powder, salt, cinnamon, ginger, nutmeg, cloves, allspice, and black pepper.

3. In a large bowl, whisk together brown sugar, egg, and egg yolk.

4. In a small saucepan, melt 3 ounces (85 grams) chocolate and butter over medium-low heat. Remove from heat, and slowly whisk into brown sugar mixture until well incorporated. Whisk in Vin Chaud, vanilla, and zest. Fold flour mixture into chocolate mixture, just until combined.

5. Divide mixture evenly between mini muffin pan wells. On a towel-lined counter, tap pan a couple of times to level batter.

6. Bake until puffed and set around the corners, 10 to 15 minutes.

7. In a small saucepan, heat cream and remaining 2 ounces (57 grams) chocolate over medium-low heat, stirring occasionally, until melted and smooth. Transfer to a piping bag and cut a ¼-inch opening. Pipe a nickel-sized amount on top of each brownie. Garnish with confectioners' sugar, if desired. Store in airtight container in refrigerator for up to 1 week. Serve at room temperature.

CHOCOLATE PEANUT BUTTER FUDGE

MAKES ABOUT 25

There is one, and only one, recipe my dad knows how to make from memory. His Chocolate Peanut Butter Fudge has been made and loved by our family since before I was born, but I'm not sure the recipe has ever been written down until now. While writing this book, my dad sent me videos of him making the fudge, and it was so helpful in getting the recipe just right to share with you. The texture of his fudge is more like a praline, not soft like what you might know from other fudge variations. You can choose crunchy or smooth peanut butter based on your preference, but the crunchy version adds texture and is what my dad uses. —Brian

INGREDIENTS

1 cup (227 grams) salted butter, plus more for dish

2 ounces (57 grams) unsweetened baking chocolate*

2 cups (480 grams) whole milk

4 cups (800 grams) granulated sugar

1 cup (240 grams) cold water (for testing)

2 teaspoons (8 grams) vanilla extract

1 cup (250 grams) extra crunchy peanut butter

DIRECTIONS

1. Butter an 8-inch square baking dish.

2. In a large saucepan, melt butter and chocolate over medium-high heat, stirring continuously, then stir in milk. Slowly add the sugar, making sure sugar does not get on sides of saucepan, and stir well until dissolved. Once all the sugar is added, bring to a boil, stirring constantly, until you drop a small amount into the cold water and it forms a soft ball (an instant read thermometer will register 240°F/115°C), about 18 minutes.

3. Remove from heat and stir in vanilla. Add peanut butter, stirring until combined, but not too long or it will set up in the dish. Pour into the prepared dish and allow to cool.

4. Once the fudge has cooled and is somewhat firm, use a sharp knife to cut into 1½-inch pieces. Store in airtight container at room temperature for up to 1 week.

We used Baker's Unsweetened Chocolate.

CHEDDAR PECAN DILL BISCUITS

MAKES 12

These are loosely based on a certain seafood chain restaurant's cheesy biscuits. The pecan and dill give them the new life they need. —B+B

INGREDIENTS

- 1½ cups (188 grams) all-purpose flour, divided
- ⅓ cup (76 grams) plus 2 tablespoons (28 grams) cold unsalted butter, divided
- ⅔ cup (74 grams) freshly grated sharp Cheddar cheese, divided
- ½ cup (57 grams) toasted chopped pecans
- 2 tablespoons (8 grams) chopped fresh dill
- 1½ teaspoons (6 grams) granulated sugar
- 1¼ teaspoons (3 grams) kosher salt, divided
- ½ teaspoon (2.5 grams) baking powder
- ½ teaspoon (1.5 grams) instant yeast
- ½ teaspoon (2.5 grams) baking soda
- ¼ teaspoon garlic powder
- ¼ teaspoon ground black pepper
- ⅔ cup (160 grams) hot whole buttermilk (120°F/49°C to 130°F/54°C)

DIRECTIONS

1. Preheat oven to 400°F (200°C). Line a rimmed baking sheet with parchment paper.

2. In a medium bowl, place ¾ cup (94 grams) flour. Cube ⅓ cup (76 grams) cold butter; add to bowl, tossing to coat. Using a pastry blender or 2 forks, cut in butter until mixture is crumbly. Stir in ⅓ cup (37 grams) cheese, pecans, and dill.

3. In a medium bowl, mix together sugar, 1 teaspoon (3 grams) salt, baking powder, yeast, baking soda, garlic powder, pepper, and remaining ¾ cup (94 grams) flour. Add hot buttermilk, stirring just until combined. Let cool for 3 to 5 minutes. Add cheese mixture; stir until a dough starts to form. (It is OK if not all flour has been fully incorporated.) Using a spatula or your hands, knead dough in bowl until just combined. Using a 2-tablespoon spring-loaded scoop, scoop dough (about 45 grams each), and drop about 1 inch apart onto prepared pan. Top with remaining ⅓ cup (37 grams) cheese.

4. Bake until lightly golden brown and cheese is melted, about 12 minutes.

5. Meanwhile, in a small saucepan, heat remaining 2 tablespoons (28 grams) butter, and remaining ¼ teaspoon salt over medium heat until butter is melted. Brush hot biscuits with butter mixture and serve immediately. Best served same day.

ICED GINGERBREAD COOKIES

MAKES ABOUT 55

We normally get our first taste of gingerbread during the summer when we begin testing and tasting holiday recipes for our magazines. It might be out of season at that time, but we're always happy when it's Christmas in July and the first gingerbread cookies come out of the oven. −B+B

INGREDIENTS

1 cup (227 grams) unsalted butter, softened

¾ cup (165 grams) firmly packed dark brown sugar

¼ cup (50 grams) granulated sugar

1 large egg (50 grams), room temperataure

1½ teaspoons (6 grams) vanilla extract

¼ cup (85 grams) unsulphured molasses

3 cups (375 grams) all-purpose flour

2 teaspoons (4 grams) ground cinnamon

1½ teaspoons (7.5 grams) baking powder

1 teaspoon (2 grams) ground ginger

¾ teaspoon (2.25 grams) kosher salt

¼ teaspoon ground nutmeg

¼ teaspoon ground cloves

Gingerbread Cookie Icing (recipe on page 131)

DIRECTIONS

1. In the bowl of a stand mixer fitted with the paddle attachment, beat butter and sugars at medium speed until creamy, 3 to 4 minutes, stopping to scrape sides of bowl. Beat in egg and vanilla until combined. Beat in molasses just until combined, stopping to scrape sides of bowl.

2. In a medium bowl, whisk together flour, cinnamon, baking powder, ginger, salt, nutmeg, and cloves. With mixer on low speed, gradually add flour mixture to butter mixture, beating just until combined and stopping to scrape sides of bowl as needed. (Dough will be slightly sticky.)

3. On a lightly floured surface, divide dough into 2 portions (480 grams each). Shape into disks, wrap in plastic wrap, and refrigerate until firm, about 1 hour.

4. Preheat oven to 375°F (190°C). Line baking sheets with parchment paper.

5. On a lightly floured surface, roll one portion of dough to ¼-inch thickness. (Keep remaining dough refrigerated until ready to roll.) Using desired 1¾-inch holiday cutters dipped in flour, cut as many cookies as possible, rerolling scraps as needed and refrigerating dough if it becomes too soft. Place cookies 2 inches apart on prepared pans. Repeat with remaining dough portion.

6. Bake until centers are slightly puffed and dry and edges are slightly golden, 6 to 9 minutes. Let cool slightly on pans, about 3 minutes. Remove from pans, and let cool completely on wire racks. Place Gingerbread Cookie Icing in piping bag fitted with a coupler to switch between tips, as desired (Wilton #1 and #2). Decorate as desired with Gingerbread Cookie Icing. Store in an airtight container at room temperature for up to 2 weeks.

CHEDDAR PECAN CRACKERS

MAKES ABOUT 38

Puh-KAHN or PEE-can? The pronunciation might be up for conversation, but the ingredient isn't. These addictive crackers get a double dose of pecans. —B+B

INGREDIENTS

- 1½ cup (188 grams) all-purpose flour
- ½ cup (61 grams) pecan flour*
- 1 teaspoon (3 grams) kosher salt
- ½ teaspoon (1 gram) garlic powder
- ½ teaspoon (1 gram) ground red pepper
- 2½ cups (250 grams) finely shredded sharp Cheddar cheese, room temperature
- 6 tablespoons (84 grams) unsalted butter, cubed and softened
- 38 pecan halves* (94 grams)
- Flaky sea salt, for sprinkling

DIRECTIONS

1. In the bowl of a stand mixer fitted with the paddle attachment, add all-purpose flour, pecan flour, salt, garlic powder, and red pepper. Mix on low speed until combined. Add cheese and butter, and beat on medium-low speed until combined and a soft dough forms and holds together when squeezed in your hands, about 4 minutes.

2. Shape dough into a 9½-inch log, about 1½ inches in diameter. Wrap in plastic wrap and chill in the refrigerator until firm, at least 1 hour or up to overnight.

3. Preheat oven to 375°F (190°C). Line two baking sheets with parchment paper.

4. Using a sharp knife, cut log into ¼-inch thick slices. Place on prepared baking sheet. Press a pecan half on the top of each cracker. Sprinkle with flaky sea salt.

5. Bake until edges are lightly browned, 14 to 16 minutes, rotating halfway through. Allow to cool on the pan for at least 5 minutes before moving to a wire rack to cool completely. Store in an airtight container at room temperature for up to 2 weeks.

We used Schermer Pecans pecan flour and pecans.

FIG AND ROSEMARY CRACKERS

MAKES ABOUT 30

(Photo on page 128)

These thinly sliced crackers are big on flavor and crunch. They're reminiscent of a goat cheese-rosemary spread I used to make that was a perfect vehicle for serving my homemade fig preserves I'd put up each summer. —*Brooke*

INGREDIENTS

- ½ cup (63 grams) all-purpose flour
- ½ cup (65 grams) whole-wheat flour
- 2 tablespoons (8 grams) fresh rosemary leaves, coarsely chopped
- 1 teaspoon (5 grams) baking soda
- ½ teaspoon (1.5 grams) kosher salt
- ½ cup (90 grams) dried black mission figs, chopped
- ¼ cup (35 grams) whole hazelnuts, coarsely chopped
- 1 cup (240 grams) whole milk
- 2 tablespoons (42 grams) honey

DIRECTIONS

1. Preheat oven to 350°F (180°C). Lightly spray an 8½x4½-inch loaf pan with baking spray with flour.

2. In a large bowl, mix together flours, rosemary, baking soda, and salt. Add figs and hazelnuts.

3. In a small bowl, whisk together milk and honey until combined. Slowly add to the dry ingredients and stir until just combined. Pour batter into prepared loaf pan.

4. Bake until golden and set, about 20 minutes. Allow to cool in the pan for 10 minutes before removing; remove from pan, and let cool completely on a wire rack. Wrap in plastic wrap and freeze until firm, 1 to 2 hours, or until ready to use.

5. Preheat oven to 325°F (170°C). Line a sheet pan with parchment paper.

6. Using a large, serrated knife, slice the loaf into ⅛-inch thick slices. Place cut side down on prepared pan.

7. Bake until crackers are golden, about 10 minutes. Remove pan from oven and carefully turn crackers over. Continue to bake until crackers are crispy and dried, 15 to 20 minutes more. Allow to cool on pan for 10 minutes; remove to a wire rack, and let cool completely. Store in an airtight container at room temperature for up to 1 week.

GINGERBREAD COOKIE ICING

MAKES ABOUT 2½ CUPS

INGREDIENTS	DIRECTIONS
3¾ cups (450 grams) confectioners' sugar 2½ tablespoons (25 grams) meringue powder 6 tablespoons (90 grams) warm water (105°F/41°C to 110°F/43°C)	1. In the bowl of a stand mixer fitted with the paddle attachment, beat confectioners' sugar and meringue powder at low speed until combined. Slowly add 6 tablespoons (90 grams) warm water, beating until fluid, about 1 minute. Increase mixer speed to medium, and beat until stiff, 4 to 5 minutes. Use immediately and cover with a wet cloth when not using to keep from setting up. Store in an airtight container for up to 3 days.

ROUGH PUFF PASTRY DOUGH

MAKES ENOUGH FOR 14 MINI ECCLES CAKES

INGREDIENTS	DIRECTIONS
1⅓ cups (300 grams) cold unsalted butter, cubed 2¼ cups (281 grams) all-purpose flour 2 teaspoons (6 grams) kosher salt ½ cup (120 grams) ice water	1. Freeze butter until firm, 15 to 20 minutes. 2. In the bowl of a stand mixer fitted with the paddle attachment, beat frozen butter, flour, and salt at low speed just until butter is coated with flour. With mixer on low speed, add ½ cup (120 grams) ice water in a slow, steady stream, beating just until dough comes together, about 1 minute, stopping to scrape sides of bowl, and turn dough to help dough hydrate evenly. (There will still be large pieces of butter. It is OK if a few dry bits remain). 3. Turn out dough onto a lightly floured surface, and roll into a 7-inch square. Wrap in plastic wrap, and refrigerate for 45 minutes to 1 hour. 4. On a lightly floured surface, roll dough into an 18×10-inch rectangle, lightly flouring surface and top of dough as needed. Fold dough in thirds like a letter. Rotate dough 90 degrees; roll into an 18×10-inch rectangle, and fold in thirds like a letter. Repeat procedure for a third and final time. Wrap dough in plastic wrap, and refrigerate for at least 1 hour. (If at any point the butter is too soft after a fold, wrap in plastic wrap, and freeze until butter is firm again, checking every 5 minutes).

To my husband, Stephen, no one makes a Manhattan better than you do. And while you thought I was adapting your recipe for this book… surprise! Your recipe is included. Because it's that good and should be enjoyed year-round.

Forever, my work will be dedicated to my mom, Phyllis Hoffman DePiano, who passed away as the first edition of this book was on press. She never saw the surprise that awaited her on page 86, but she knew the love and laughter that that recipe represents to us. That Brandy Alexander was photographed in her crystal coupe glasses that she passed down to me a few years ago when I published my very first cocktail book, *The Coupe*. They will be cherished for the rest of my life, and I will raise a glass to her each time I use them. I love you, Mom! —*Brian*

To my husband, Andy, for always having a cocktail waiting on me when I walk in the door at the end of the day. I adore our cocktail hours together.

To my mom, the talent behind Bobbins Design, for making cocktail hours everywhere beautiful with monogrammed linens. —*Brooke*

INDEX

RESOURCES & NOTES

Page 5: Antique Brass Cocktail Picks available at Williams Sonoma

Page 12: Coupe glasses in mint green available at Estelle Colored Glass; copper champagne bowl available at Mauviel

Page 19: Sferra cocktail napkins and custom monogram available at Bobbins Design

Page 20: Circa Coupe Glasses available at Shop Hammett

Page 24: Custom cocktail napkins available at Courtland & Co.

Pages 28 – 29: Sferra and Tina Chen cocktail napkins and custom monogram available at Bobbins Design

Page 33: Cocktail napkin by Sferra; Williams Sonoma x Billy Reid coupe glasses and jigger available at Williams Sonoma

Page 34: Williams Sonoma x Billy Reid Cocktail Napkins available at Williams Sonoma

Page 38: Cocktail napkin by Sferra; Rialto Coupe Glass in Limoncello available at Shop Hammett

Page 41: Tulia Coupe Glass available at Brooke & Lou; cocktail napkins available at Bobbins Design

Page 42: Sferra cocktail napkins available at Bobbins Design; Imperial Glass Candlewick Coupe available at Replacements

Page 45: Williams Sonoma x Billy Reid Cocktail mixing glass and bar spoon available at Williams Sonoma; Quinn citrine coupe glasses available at Caskata; Williams Sonoma x Billy Reid pitcher and stirring spoon available at Williams Sonoma

Page 46: Sferra cocktail napkins and custom monogram available at Bobbins Design

Page 49: Sferra cocktail napkins; custom monogram available at Bobbins Design

Page 57: Tina Chen cocktail napkin and custom monogram available at Bobbins Design; Ramona Coupe Glass in Peach available at Anthropologie

Page 58: Cocktail Napkin by Sferra; Gorham Crystal Viscount Coupe available at Replacements

Page 61: Fostoria American Clear Coupe available at Replacements

Page 62: Champagne Theatre Saucer glasses at Shop Hammett

Page 65: Cocktail napkin by Sferra; Gold Rocher coupe available at Lucy's Market

Page 66: Felix Optic Coupe available at Crate & Barrel

Page 69: Cocktail Napkin by Sferra; Pryce Gold Coupe available at Crate & Barrel

Page 75: Etched Coupe available at Crate & Barrel; Crown Linens cocktail napkins available at Bobbins Design

Page 76: Liberta Stemmed Glass in Clear and Bilboa Cocktail Napkins available at Shop Hammett

Page 79: Cocktail napkin by Sferra

Page 83: Cocktail napkins by Sferra; coupe glasses available at Replacements

Page 84: Lenox Monroe Coupe available at Replacements

Page 87: Brass cocktail shaker and Marble and Brass Bar Tool Set available at Williams Sonoma; Cocktail gasses available at Replacements

Page 88: Custom cocktail napkins available at Courtland & Co.; Coupe glass available Williams Sonoma

Page 97: Cocktail napkin by Sferra; Coupe glass available at Replacements

Page 98: Williams Sonoma x Billy Reid Cocktail Napkins available at Williams Sonoma

Page 101: Cocktail Napkins by Sferra; Lenox Aria Coupe available at Replacements

Page 102: Tiffin-Franciscan Westchester Coupe available at Replacements

Page 105: Cocktail napkin by Sferra, Williams Sonoma x Billy Reid coupe glass

Page 106: Cocktail napkin by Sferra

Page 111: Coupe Glasses in Emerald Green available at Estelle Colored Glass

Page 116: Circa Coupe Glass in Peach available at Shop Hammett; cocktail napkin by Sferra

Page 128: Tree serving board available at Williams Sonoma; Williams Sonoma x Billy Reid coupe glass available at Williams Sonoma; Haute Home cocktail napkins available at Bobbins Design

---

Anthropologie: *anthropologic.com*

Bobbins Design: *bobbinsdesign.com*

Brooke & Lou: *brookeandlou.com*

Caskata: *caskata.com*

Courtland & Co.: *courtlandandco.com*

Crate & Barrel: *crateandbarrel.com*

Estelle Colored Glass: *estellecoloredglass.com*

Lucy's Market: *lucysmarket.com*

Mauviel: *mauviel.com*

Replacements: *replacements.com*

Sferra: *sferra.com*

Shop Hammett: *shophammett.com*

Williams Sonoma: *williams-sonoma.com*

CREDITS:

Editorial Director: Anna Hartzog

Sr. Administrative Art Director: Tracy Wood-Franklin

Art Director: Jennifer Compton

Test Kitchen Director: Laura Crandall

Photographer: Kyle Carpenter

Food Stylists / Food Recipe Developers: Katie Moon Dickerson, Vanessa Rocchio, Amanda Stabile, and Izzie Turner

Prop Stylists: Mary Beth Jones, Maggie Hill

Copy Editor: Kellie Keeling

Imaging Specialist: Delisa McDaniel